TEXAS

THE LAND ▲ THE PEOPLE ▲ THE CITIES

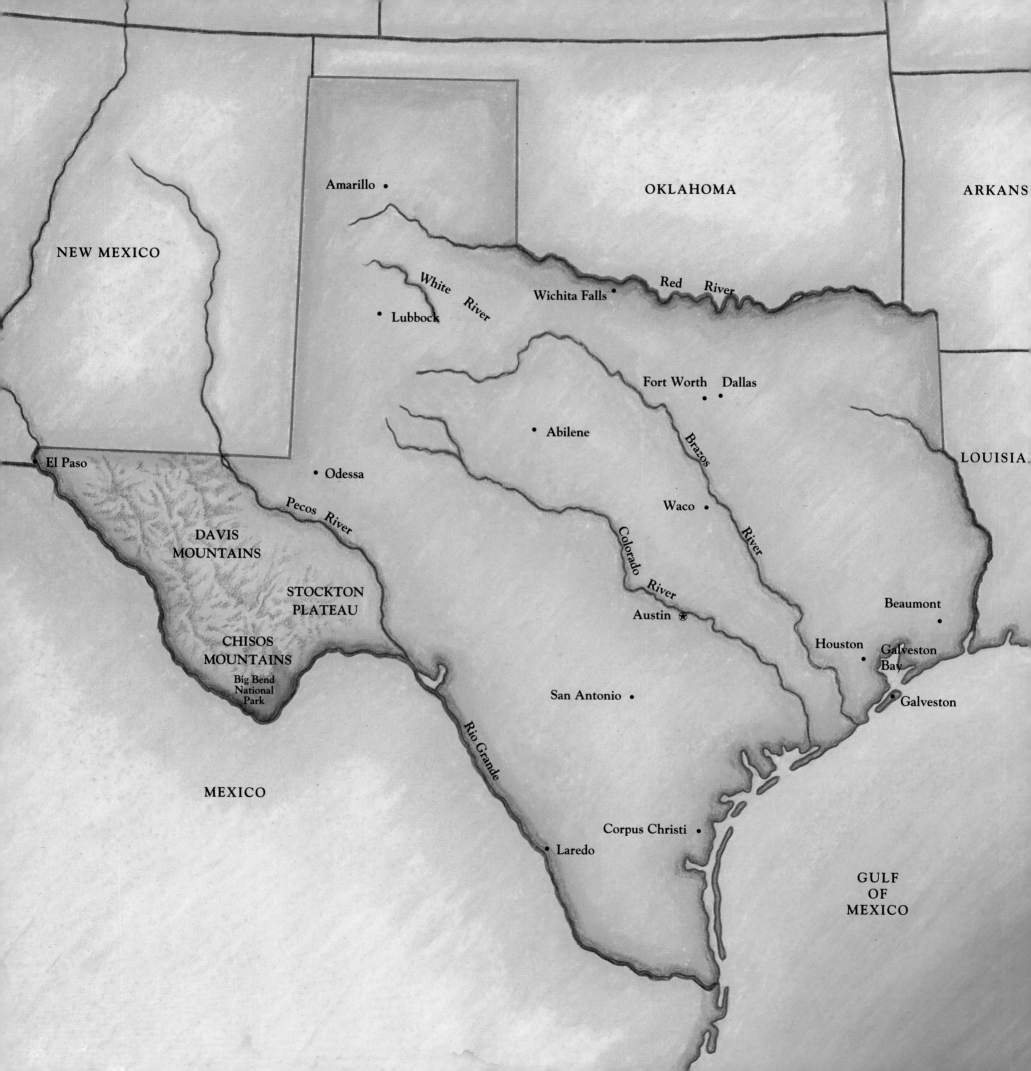

TEXAS

THE LAND ▲ THE PEOPLE ▲ THE CITIES

GARY REYES

PHOTOGRAPHY BY
JOE VIESTI

MALLARD PRESS

MALLARD PRESS
AN IMPRINT OF BDD PROMOTIONAL BOOK COMPANY, INC.
666 FIFTH AVENUE ▲ NEW YORK ▲ NEW YORK 10103

A FRIEDMAN GROUP BOOK

Published by MALLARD PRESS
An imprint of BDD Promotional Book Company, Inc.
666 Fifth Avenue
New York, New York 10103

Mallard Press and its accompanying design and logo are trademarks of BDD
Promotional Book Company, Inc.

ISBN 0-7924-5302-6

TEXAS
The Land, The People, The Cities
was prepared and produced by
Michael Friedman Publishing Group, Inc.
15 West 26th Street
New York, New York 10010

Editor: Sharyn Rosart
Designer: Stephanie Bart-Horvath
Photography Editor: Christopher C. Bain
Additional Photo Research: Anne K. Price
All photographs © Joe Viesti 1991.

Typeset by The Interface Group, Inc.
Color separations by Scantrans Pte. Ltd.
Printed and bound in Hong Kong by Leefung-Asco Printers Ltd.

To my mother,
a living Yellow Rose of Texas

CONTENTS

THE LAND
8

THE PEOPLE
52

THE CITIES
82

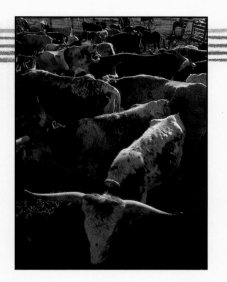

THE LAND

Perhaps more than anything else, the land itself is what gives the state of Texas its unique character. Larger than all the other American states except Alaska, and larger than many countries around the world, the vast size of Texas has helped to define the state, and has contributed to the strong and independent nature of its people and cities. Stretching over seven hundred miles (1,126 km) across ten degrees of longitude, and over eight hundred miles (1,287 km) across thirteen degrees of latitude, Texas sits in two time zones and is separated by only a few hundred miles from a third. It occupies about 7 percent of the total water and land area of the United States. In elevation, Texas ranges from sea level to over 8,000 feet (2,400 m). In short, the state is big. In its brief but storied history, the land under the feet of native Texans has fueled big wealth, big egos, and above all else, big dreams.

From Colony to State

Well before the Pilgrims arrived in Plymouth, another group of Europeans found their way to modern-day Texas. In the early sixteenth century, the Spaniard Alonzo Alvarez de Piñeda, on behalf of the Catholic Church, led an expedition up what is now called the Texas Gulf Coast. He was followed several years later by his countryman Cabeza de Vaca. While both expeditions proved somewhat futile (de Vaca was actually shipwrecked on Galveston Island), they did serve to spread false but alluring tales of great wealth. Those tales resulted in subsequent and repeated expeditions to the mainland of modern-day Texas.

By the late seventeenth century, French expansion west of the Louisiana Territories began to encroach on land controlled by Spain. In part as a defensive measure, Spain embarked on a period of rapid growth of its mission and fortress development throughout what is now the Texas region. For the most part, Spain's efforts to buttress its position in the region were successful, thwarting further French development upon land in Texas controlled by the Spanish empire.

In 1821, Mexico accomplished what the French had been unable to do. When Mexico gained its independence from Spain, the new country also obtained control over the lands North of the Rio Grande River that had been previously held by the Spanish. All at once, Texas left the protective arms of a great European power and assumed its place as a state in the newly independent Republic of Mexico. Its status in the sphere of Mexican influence was shaky from the start, however. The ill-defined boundaries resulting from the American purchase of the Louisiana Territories in 1803 created a most enticing atmosphere for American settlement in the Texas region. In fact, during the years immediately following the Louisiana Purchase, the majority of settlers in the Texas area came from the United States.

In 1825, U.S. President John Quincy Adams offered the Republic of Mexico one million dollars for the land within the vaguely defined boundaries

THE BARREN BUT
dramatic peaks of Guadalupe
Mountains National Park
reach into the blue sky of Western Texas (page 8).

THE GUADALUPE MOUN-
tains National Park sits just on
the Texas side of the border
with New Mexico and contains
Guadalupe Peak. At just over
eight thousand seven hundred
feet (2,600 m), Guadalupe Peak
is the highest point in Texas.

TEXANS REMEMBER THE
Alamo, the spirit and pride
their battles there instilled in
them forever.

of Texas. Although the Mexican government refused the offer, U.S. citizens continued to settle in Texas, since the physical barriers to entry were easily overcome. Over the course of the early 1830s, momentum built rapidly for the formation of a Texas independent of Mexican rule. In response to a formal declaration of independence by the newly elected government of the Republic of Texas, Mexican President Antonio Lopez de Santa Anna led a potent army of several thousand men on a mission to crush the independence movement and its backers. At the Alamo in San Antonio, Santa Anna and his army encountered spirited resistance from a defense force of less than two hundred men and women. Although he was able to endure and rout the rag-tag band of volunteers, and continue his march toward the headquarters of the upstart republic, the stage had been set for Santa Anna's eventual defeat. History and legend have well recorded the events of April 1836, when a rough and disorganized band of volunteers, led by Sam Houston, made quick and decisive work of Santa Anna's army at San Jacinto.

With that victory, Texas was able to establish itself as a sovereign nation, recognized by the United States and by many European nations as an independent and self-supporting member of the world community. Although its status as an independent nation would last only ten years, after which it would become the twenty-eighth state of the United States of America, the decade of the Republic of Texas would serve to forever instill a sense of deep-rooted pride and independence in all who call themselves Texans.

▲   ▲   ▲   ▲

Entry into the union of American states gave Texas distinct and clearly defined boundaries for the first time in its history. Within those boundaries lay an expansive and incredibly diverse land stretching

THE MAMMOTH CAVES OF Seminole Canyon State Park sit at the foot of the West Texas desert.

THE BEAUTY AND CHARM OF the Texas Hill Country make it the home of choice for many artists, musicians, and craftsmen.

from the American South to the mostly unexplored American West. Although the geographic boundaries of Texas were permanently fixed with entry into the United States, the cultural boundaries remained dynamic and ever changing. This was in large part due to the physical makeup of the land itself. Within the new boundaries of America's twenty-eighth state, five distinct land regions coexisted, each infusing its own unique physical characteristics into the lives of its inhabitants.

East Texas

The swamplands and forests of East Texas lend themselves to comparison with the American South. Indeed, the Piney Woods and Big Thicket regions of East Texas extend the physical and psychological boundaries of the South across the

Sabine River into the Lone Star state. This easternmost region of Texas is home to an abundance of plant and animal life that thrives in the channels and bayous of the area's many lakes and rivers. Indeed, the boundaries of East Texas are themselves defined by bodies of water, with the Red River on the north, the Sabine River on the east, and the Gulf of Mexico to the south. Contained within this area of over 50,000 square miles (130,000 square km) is by far the most extensive and diverse collection of flora and fauna that the state of Texas has to offer. Fed by three of the state's great rivers (the Sabine, the Neches, and the Trinity), the natural and manmade lakes of East Texas provide a source of food and energy to a diverse mixture of wildlife.

Caddo Lake, near Marshall in the far northeastern corner of the state, is a sportsman's dream as well as a popular backdrop for professional and

THE DAVY CROCKETT
National Forest spreads its
thicket over four hundred
square miles (650 square km) of
East Texas. The region's forests
are marked by their mixture of
evergreen and hardwood trees.

THE BALD EAGLE IS A RARE SIGHT TO most Americans, but a familiar friend to residents of the Highland Lakes region of Central Texas.

IN A STATE AS BIG AND DIVERSE AS TEXAS, ONE CAN TRAVEL THROUGH A multitude of ecologic zones. Gorman Falls (pictured) brings the look of a tropical rain forest to Central Texas.

WHEN FALL ARRIVES, MANY *are drawn to the Piney Woods region of East Texas, and to the dramatic color of its forests and thickets. The abundance of maple, oak, and gum trees ensures that fall color seekers will not be disappointed.*

amateur photographers. Dam construction along the Sabine River and the Trinity River has provided fishermen with a never-ending supply of fish, and of fish stories, in Toledo Bend Reservoir and Lake Livingston. The latter, an immense freshwater paradise stretching for more than twenty-five miles (40 km) near Huntsville, Texas, draws five million visitors a year to its shorelines and recreation areas. The other lakes of East Texas provide a bounty of trophy-sized fish, including black bass, pike, and catfish.

Out of the water, the area's forests provide nesting and breeding habitats for a wide variety of birds, including the great blue heron, the wood duck, and the ruby-throated hummingbird. Animals that thrive in the dual land-and-marine environment, such as alligators and tree frogs, are also found in abundance.

While the lakes and rivers of East Texas give the region its soul, the forests and thickets give it character. By closing off large parts of the East Texas forests to commercial exploitation, the state of Texas has preserved the beauty and charm that nature has cultivated over many generations. Hundreds of varieties of trees grow tall in protected areas such as the Davy Crockett and Sam Houston National Forests. Evergreens abound, but they are only one example of the glorious variety of trees to be found in East Texas. Hardwoods such as birch and walnut also thrive. With the year-round beauty of the Spanish cypress, the majesty of the dozen or so varieties of oak, and the colorful explosion of maple in the fall, the Piney Woods of Texas stand up against any region in the country for diversity and beauty.

In addition to enjoying the natural beauty, hunting, fishing, and camping on a year-round basis, natives and visitors to East Texas can experience one of the many annual festivals in the region, such as the Texas Renaissance Festival in Plantersville.

North Texas

The rich and fertile earth of the American Midwest has brought an agrarian life-style into the Texas heartland as well. The dark and nutrient-rich soils of

YOU NEVER KNOW WHERE THE LONE STAR OF THE TEXAS FLAG WILL TURN UP!

*A SIMPLE HOME NESTLED
in the Texas hills is paradise to
many devoted Texans.*

THE LONE STAR FEED-
yard in Happy, Texas, is one of
many in the state that fatten
the cattle before they go to market or to auction. Grain-fed cattle bring a higher price than do
range-fed cattle.

EVEN WITH THOUSANDS OF
cattle ranches across the state,
each ranch's distinct brand
helps insure that strays will
always find their way home.

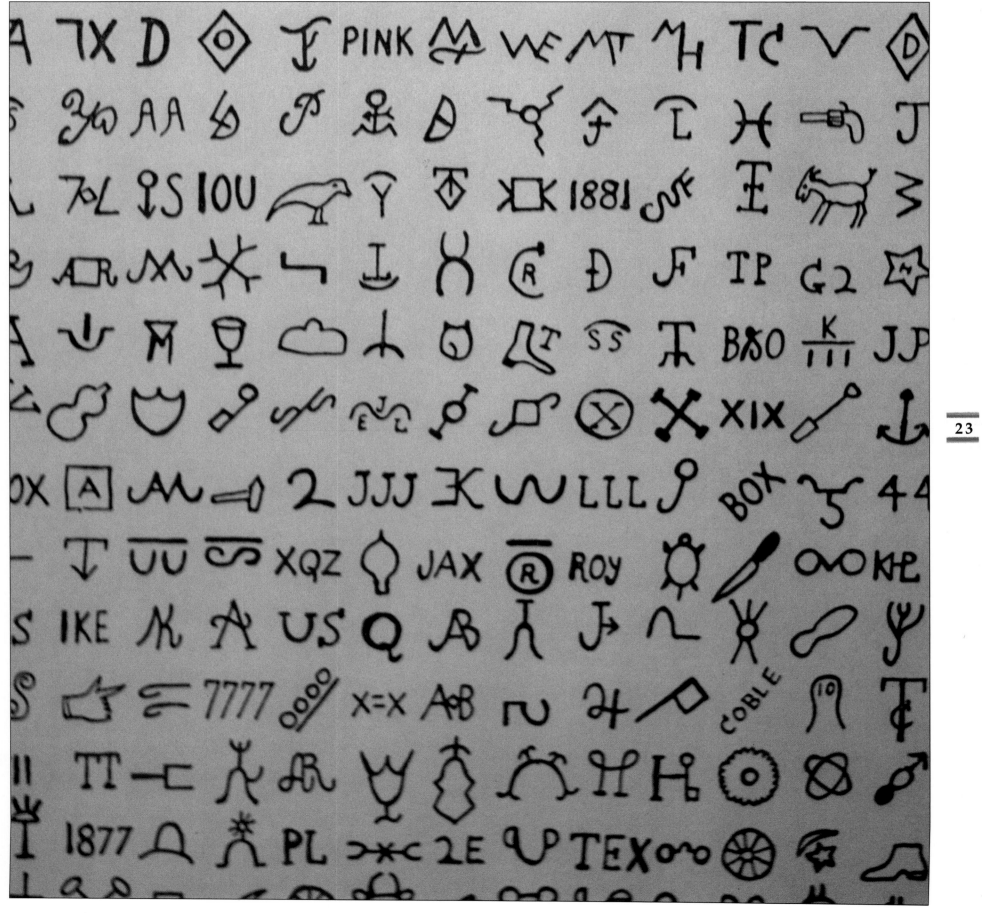

EFFORTS HAVE BEEN MADE on various ranches across the state to preserve the buffalo, at one time a prosperous and plentiful roamer of the High Plains.

North Central Texas have given birth to unrivaled agricultural kingdoms. The multitude of cotton and grain farms scattered across northern Texas have helped clothe and feed the world for over one hundred years while simultaneously giving the state a solid moral foundation on which to build its character. With the land providing the soil, and the Spanish missionaries providing the seeds and planting expertise, the cultivation and harvesting of wheat began in Texas more than four hundred years ago and continues today. The state's moderate weather conditions lend themselves to an almost continual harvest of wheat and other grains. Beginning in the central part of the state around the middle of May, and moving northward through the late summer and early fall months, bountiful grain harvests keep silos and mills full on an almost year-round basis. In fact, the state of Texas now ranks third in the country in the production of winter wheat, with over eight million acres (3.2 million ha) of land committed. In addition to being a strong economic generator in and

of itself, the production of home-grown wheat also contributes to the state's unrivaled status in cattle raising and beef production.

Texas is also a major grower of cotton, wheat, rice, and other grains and cereals, plus corn, peanuts, and soybeans. Generations of farmers, beginning with Native Americans and Spanish missionaries, then moving on to western pioneers and settlers, must be credited with providing the human capital necessary for turning the fertile lands of Texas into a bounty of commercial bonanzas. They planted the values of rural America in Texas. Rural education, religious institutions, and a work ethic second to none, are but a few of the human crops cultivated and harvested by the agricultural community. Ultimately, however, it is the land and its soil that are responsible for bringing the values, beliefs, and dreams of the American heartland into Texas. Loss or destruction of the land through over-development and pollution will mean the end of Texas' widely respected rural values.

THE L.B.J. RANCH, WHICH stretches across hundreds of acres in Central Texas, is the final resting ground for former president, and favorite son of Texas, Lyndon Baines Johnson.

The Panhandle

The canyons and plateaus of the Texas Panhandle extend southward the regional influence of the American High Plains. Named for its shape, the Texas Panhandle extends south from the state's northernmost boundary with Oklahoma for more than three hundred miles (483 km) along the border with New Mexico. For more than ten thousand years, this region of Texas has been inhabited by Native Americans who have sustained themselves by hunting the small animals that occupy the grassy plains and small lakes. The Panhandle's harsh climate, with its cold winters followed by hot and dry summers, kept American settlers away until the middle of the nineteenth century. When settlers did arrive, the vast and fertile plains of the Panhandle soon proved themselves receptive to farming and ranching, thereby setting events in motion for the wide-scale population and settlement of the region.

While many of the ranching and farming empires of Texas call the Panhandle home, the region's greatest tourist assets are the Palo Duro and Llano Estacado canyons. Named for the juniper trees that grow on the canyon walls (the words *palo duro* are thought to mean "hard wood"), the deep gorges of Palo Duro Canyon are several hundred million years old. Visitors to the fifteen-thousand-acre (6,000-ha) Palo Duro Canyon State Park can witness the geologic development of the earth as it is revealed in the layers of sediment of the canyon walls. Roughly the same age as the Grand Canyon, Palo Duro Canyon displays Earth's history in layers of sandstone, shale, clay, and gypsum. The oldest exposed rock in the canyon is over two hundred million years old. Subsequent, "younger," formations rise from the canyon floor and range in age from many millions of years to just a few hundred thousand years. The deep walls, which shield the canyon from harsh weather, provide a major source of materials used in the pottery and toolmaking of Native Americans. The cottonwood, mesquite, and juniper trees that dot the region add a splash of color to the earthen hues of the canyon floor.

THE SECRET TO DETER-
mining the geologic age of
Texas is found in the sedemen-
tary rock of Palo Duro Canyon
State Park near Amarillo.
Thorough examination of the
canyon floor reveals that Texas
should be celebrating its two-
hundred-fifty-millionth birth-
day, give or take a few million
years.

29

THE NATIVE AMERICAN PICTOGRAPHS FOUND IN
the caves of Seminole Canyon State Park offer visitors
a vision of what life in Texas was like well before
European settlement.

A SURE SIGN THAT SPRING *has arrived in Texas is the blanket of bluebonnets that lays over fields across the state. Although bluebonnets grow wild in Texas, picking them is prohibited because of their status as the official state flower.*

UNDER A BIG SKY, THE *Ranch Heritage Center in Lubbock displays the tools and methods used by previous generations in the settling of the Texas Panhandle.*

West Texas

At the foot of the Panhandle lies the vast western portion of Texas, an area of the state that epitomizes the isolation and beauty of the American desert. From the edge of the metropolitan area of El Paso, the West Texas desert stretches over four hundred miles (640 km) into the heart of the state. From the river beds of the Rio Grande River, which form the southwestern boundary of the state, to the top of Guadalupe Peak, at 8,749 feet (2,625 m), the highest point in Texas, the desert offers a striking contrast to the other regions of the state. Nowhere are the wonders of this desert more in evidence than in Big Bend National Park. Nestled along a cusp in the Rio Grande River, Big Bend National Park is home to several mountain ranges and to an impressive variety of desert flora and fauna. With over sixty varieties of cacti alone, the park serves a vital role as a living laboratory. Plants such as the creosote bush, with its thirty-foot (9-m) taproot, and the candelilla, with its waxy coating that preserves water, offer biologists a peak into nature's secrets of adaptation to harsh climates. While rains are few and far between in the desert, the two hundred or so springs and seeps collect and retain enough water to support a thriving population of doves, deer, and bobcats. The rains, although infrequent, come often enough to allow for the proliferation of cottonwood trees and desert willows. While the one thousand square miles (2,600 square km) of Big Bend National Park are but a small fraction of the vast western portion of Texas, the state's extremely conscientious efforts to maintain the park's pristine condition make Big Bend an unbeatable representative of the varied and fascinating life of the desert as a whole.

WHILE MODERN TECHNOL-ogy has replaced many frontier innovations, the cowpoke's favorite mode of transporta-tion will always be the horse.

*EVEN FROM SUCH AN UNFRIENDLY LOOKING PLANT AS THE CACTUS, SPRING
in the West Texas desert brings the beauty of flowers such as the claret cup.*

THE PURPLE PRICKLY PEAR
is more enjoyable to look at
than it is to eat. Like most
cacti, the purple prickly pear
has adapted to the dry desert
conditions by developing a
waxy coat that allows it to
seal in precious moisture.

FROM EL PASO TO Brownsville, the border between Texas and Mexico is etched in the land by the waters of the Rio Grande River.

*GALVESTON'S GLORIOUS
maritime history is kept alive
with the restoration of sea-
going vessels such as the
Elissa. Fully restored and com-
pletely operational, the four
hundred-ton (360-metric ton)
sailing ship is now a permanent resident of Galveston,
courtesy of the Galveston
Historical Foundation.*

With a coastline over three hundred miles (483 km) long, Texas also has a rich maritime character, with the Gulf of Mexico providing an endless bounty of food, as well as a means of transporting to the rest of the world the goods manufactured in Texas. Padre Island National Seashore, stretching south from Corpus Christi for more than eighty miles (129 km), shows visitors a protected oasis of marine plant and animal life. Named for the island's first permanent resident, Padre Jose Nicolas Balli, a Portuguese priest who established a ranch on the island in the early 1800s, the barrier island was once the domain of the Karankawa Indians. No more than a half a mile (.8 km) across at its widest point, Padre Island separates the Gulf of Mexico from the "Mother Lake," the Laguna Madre, an inland waterway housing a plethora of delicate marine life. The Laguna Madre provides protected breeding and birthing waters for a wide variety of fish and shell-fish, including redfish, flounder, trout, and oysters. The waters of the Laguna Madre also provided the pirate Jean Lafitte with a hideaway during his reign of terror.

The construction of the first causeway connecting Padre Island to the Texas mainland, in 1927, opened the island up to development. Today, Padre Island is a first-class resort, offering vacationers a multitude of hotel and condominium choices, as well as a great variety of leisure activities. While the look of the island has changed over the years, its character and charm have not. Port Isabel, at the southern tip of the island, is home to the largest shrimper fleet in the United States and is also the point of departure for sport fishermen in search of sailfish, blue marlin, and other trophy catches in the Gulf of Mexico. The spirit of the people who inhabit the island is equally large. One resident is the dedicated Ila Loetscher, more popularly known as the "Turtle Lady," who fights to preserve endangered sea turtles and the sand dunes in which they lay their eggs. She provides a fine example of the character required if man is to live in harmony with a delicate marine ecosystem.

41

THE CRACK OF DAWN FINDS *a lone fisherman on the banks of the Rio Grande River. The two man-made lakes created from the river's water, Lake Amistad near Del Rio, and Falcon Lake near Laredo, offer some of the best fishing in the state.*

THE LIVELIHOOD OF MANY WHO LIVE ALONG THE TEXAS GULF COAST IS TIED
to the daily voyages of the shrimper fleets from Aransas Pass and other coastal
communities. Texas leads the nation in the harvesting of shrimp in the gulf.

Resources

All in all, the state of Texas sprawls over 275,000 square miles (712,250 square km) of land. To a large extent, the land has given the past and present inhabitants of Texas everything they have needed to sustain themselves and to provide for the welfare of future generations. Yet perhaps the land's most significant gift, that which is most associated with Texas, is oil.

When oil was struck in Southeast Texas near the turn of the century, the state's fate was in many ways sealed for decades to come. The oil and gas fields of East Texas were bountiful and held the potential to bring vast fortunes to the individuals who set out to harvest them, plus increased wealth for the state and its citizens as a whole. This "black gold" that spewed forth from beneath the surface fueled the growth of Texas in an exponential way. Human, as well as technological, resources were drawn to the state in large numbers, lured by the promise of fortunes waiting to be made in the oil business. Exploration for oil gave rise to an indigenous industry built on technological expertise unsurpassed in the world. The expertise needed to harvest, refine, and transport oil created a new kind of empire.

Fortunes from the Texas oil fields put money in Texas banks, which in turn put money into Texas communities. The philanthropic gestures of oil-based fortunes have served to create first-class artistic expression through endowments and direct gifts to symphonies, ballet and opera companies, and a variety of museums. Most importantly, the riches of newly discovered petroleum resources in West Texas have provided a permanent source of funding for higher education in the state.

While resources from beneath the surface have given Texas its great wealth, the abundance of land itself has been an almost equally important bounty. The rich soils of northern Texas have proven themselves fertile ground for the development of agricultural kingdoms built around cash crops such as cotton, as well as staple crops such as grains and market produce. Enterprising Texans have even

THE "BLACK-GOLD diggers" of yesteryear are on display at the Permian Basin Petroleum Museum in Midland.

EVEN ROUGH-AND-TUMBLE OIL-FIELD WORKERS HAVE A SENSE OF ARTISTIC humor in Texas.

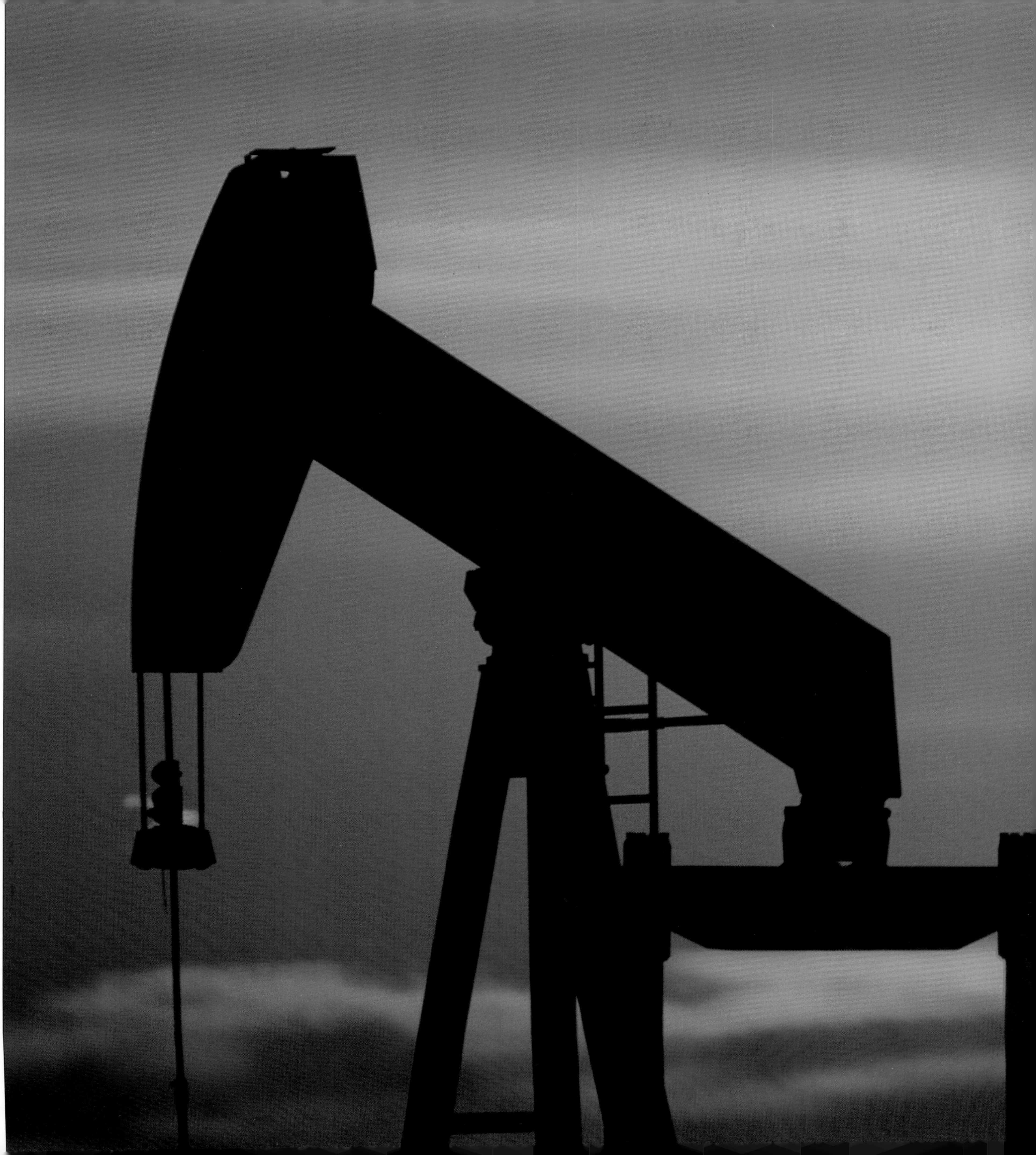

FOR MANY YEARS, THE SUN *has risen and set over the liquid fortunes trapped beneath the surface of the Texas soil.*

47

ONE OF THE MANY NOTABLE aspects of the sprawling Y.O. Ranch is its herd of Texas Longhorn cattle. The ranch, covering vast acreage in Central and West Texas, has also gained notoriety for its efforts to expose Texas schoolchildren to the great outdoors.

48

been able to capitalize on the vast amounts of nutrient-poor soils located in South and West Texas by forming a cattle and livestock empire unrivaled in the world. The seemingly endless spreads of legendary ranches, such as the King and the Y.O., have helped lead Texas to the forefront of beef production in the United States. As with the fortunes reaped from oil, the great wealth created by agribusiness in Texas has also provided for increased community development.

While efforts have been made in recent years to move away from dependence on oil and agriculture in Texas, the effort to diversify the economy is in many ways still dependent on the land on which the oil and agricultural empires were originally built.

Spirited attempts to bring to Texas industry based on advanced technologies have in large part been successful due to the abundance of cheap raw land still waiting to be put to use. The state's winning bid for the multi-billion dollar Superconducting Supercollider can be attributed equally to the efforts of political and business leaders and to the near-perfect geologic composition of the land itself.

Texans have drawn benefits from the land's spirit as well as from its bountiful natural resources. The endless supply of beauty and solitude has forged the self-reliant, resourceful, stubborn, and independent nature that characterizes inhabitants of the Lone Star state. To be a Texan is to be a human representative of the land itself.

THE COMMODITIES ON which many Texas empires were built and lost: cattle and oil. Despite recent efforts to diversify the state's economy, the history of twentieth-century Texas is the history of cattle and oil.

THE CROSBYTON SOLAR POWER PROJECT, NEAR LUBBOCK, WILL
help uncover the secrets of harnessing the sun's unlimited source of energy.

REMNANTS OF AMERICA'S PAST SPACE EXPLORATIONS ARE ON FULL
display at the Lyndon Johnson Space Center, near Houston. In addition to seeing the **Saturn**
V rocket, visitors to the complex can also view rocks brought back from the Moon by Apollo
astronauts, as well as training facilities for the Space Shuttle.

THE PEOPLE

When a foreigner, that is to say a non-Texan, meets a real Texan for the first time, several distinct impressions are sure to be made. Texans have been known to be loud, boastful, and sometimes even inaccurate with their facts. On occasion they are somewhat prone to exaggeration when describing the events that led to the creation of their portion of heaven on earth. Indeed, to many Texans, Texas is more than a state; it is also a state of mind.

A brief look at the history of Texas reveals the reasons behind the mentality of its people. Texas is unique in many respects, not the least of which is the state's existence as a free and independent republic before joining the United States of America. Unlike any other state in America, Texas has known six different rulers, including itself, in a brief time period spanning less than five hundred years. The flags of Spain, France, and Mexico have flown over Texas,

as have the flags of both a divided and a united America. This confluence of people with differing nationalities and cultures led to the creation of modern-day Texas. It is the flag of Texas, however, that unites this amalgamation of people into that most interesting member of the American community, the Texan.

To a person, Texans display an unrivaled sense of pride in their state. This outward, sometimes boastful, display is a direct result of the unique history of the state. The common historical thread uniting all Texans is the struggle to tame and conquer the often inhospitable environs of the Lone Star state. By the time European explorers made their way to Texas, it had already been occupied for hundreds of years by various groups of Native Americans who drew their total subsistence from what few resources the land would give them. The accomplishments of the Comanches, Kiowas, and Arapahoes in establishing early settlements on the harsh lands of western Texas set a precedent for future inhabitants to follow. From the earliest human settlements up until the present day, it has taken a certain type of person to lay claim to the title of Texan.

Early Settlers

By the early nineteenth century, the land Texas now occupies had become a popular destination for settlers from far and wide. The uncertain status of Texas jurisdiction made it a haven for people who were running from something or somebody. While the state attracted its share of individuals with less than reputable backgrounds, it also attracted persons of high moral standards who were looking for

LIKE ALL TEXANS, Houstonians take time every April to travel along Independence Trail, acknowledging the sacrifices of Sam Houston and his Army of the Republic of Texas.

HOMAGE IS PAID ON an annual basis to the men who chose "victory or death" during the battle of the Alamo. The duty of preserving the Alamo and its grounds is carried out by the Daughters of the Texas Republic.

a piece of land on which to stake their claim. At the time, the United States was barely fifty years old itself. As a result, a great many of the early American settlers of Texas were individuals of a strong and independent nature who were intent on leaving their mark on the world. While looking for a place to settle, these adventurers engaged in legendary struggles with the land and the environment, and they also encountered human resistance from the Native American and Mexican populations that had preceded them by many years. The ensuing battles for control of Texas, coupled with the constant efforts to tame the land, forever imbued the people of the state with a strong sense of pride rooted in struggle and conquest.

While all Americans celebrate the brilliance of national heroes such as Washington, Jefferson, and Lincoln, Texans hold additional celebrations to salute the founding fathers of their state. Pioneers such as Stephen F. Austin, who founded early colonies in Southeast Texas, and Samuel Houston, a native of Tennessee who rose to become the first president of the Republic of Texas, all converged on Texas at about the same time. The stature of Austin and Houston went well beyond the borders of Texas, as both conducted affairs of the state with the highest representatives of the U.S. and Mexican governments. Perhaps the heroes of the Alamo, men such as William Barret Travis, James Bowie, and David Crockett, are the most widely known to fans of Texas folklore. But it was the statesmanship of Stephen F. Austin and Sam Houston that led Texas out of its uncertain status in the world and into the orbit of American states.

In the early 1830s, when Texas was part of Mexico, Stephen F. Austin went to Mexico to request constitutional changes favorable to the American settler. He was not only rebuffed, but was placed in jail for having the gall to make such a request. Shortly thereafter, Texan settlers set up their own provisional government and issued a call for volunteers to wage war against the nation of Mexico. It was this call to arms that attracted the likes of Jim Bowie and Davy Crockett, men who came to Texas

COWBOYS PREPARE THEIR horses by the early morning light for the cattle drive ahead. Although most herds move north by truck or rail nowadays, "play" cattle drives are a popular form of entertainment for would-be cowhands.

THE TRADITIONAL Mexican rodeo, known as a **charreada,** *puts the finely tuned skills of the vaquero on display during the "Day in Old Mexico" fiesta in San Antonio.*

58

TRICKS OF THE TRADE are taught at an early age to young-but-eager cowpokes of the future. Organizations such as the Future Farmers of America, and the Texas Youth Rodeo Association, work to ensure that young Texans grow up with an appreciation for the state's history and character.

looking for a fight, and who in their deaths left a legacy of having bravely fought against insurmountable odds. The deaths of the Alamo heroes served as inspiration for Sam Houston and his army of volunteers in their quick and decisive defeat of Santa Anna and the Mexican Army at San Jacinto, near present-day Houston, in 1836. Just as Texas had had its own Declaration of Independence, it now had its own government, headed by the battle-tested general, Sam Houston. Over the course of the next ten years, Sam Houston worked toward his goal of having Texas join the nation of his birthplace. In 1846, after a decade as an independent nation, Texas became the twenty-eighth state in the United States of America.

▲ ▲ ▲ ▲

Although Texas then ceased to exist as an independent nation, Texans continued to live and behave as independent thinkers. With an overwhelming sense of self-reliance implanted in the minds of the state's inhabitants, the future of Texas as a haven for stubborn and free-spirited people was sealed. In fact, the agreements paving the way for Texas' entry into the U.S. made allowances for the further

THE TOOLS OF A SHERIFF'S trade have changed very little in the last one hundred years.

WHILE THE MISSION OF THE modern-day Texas Rangers may have changed, the men who wear the badge haven't. The select few who are chosen to represent one of the world's finest police forces are cut from the same mold as their frontier-conquering predecessors.

62

THE SEA TURTLE IS literally at home with Ila Loetscher. The "Turtle Lady" has opened her heart and home in an effort to protect the giant sea creature.

self-expression of independent-minded Texans. Although officially a state by the end of 1846, the transfer of public lands from Texas to U.S. control was specifically prohibited by the annexation agreements. Furthermore, in an agreement that has survived into modern times, the state of Texas demanded and was granted the right to divide itself into separate but equal divisions. To this day, a Texas politico or two can on occasion be heard mumbling on about dividing the state into four parts, thereby quadrupling the size of the Texas delegation in the U.S. Senate and, theoretically, quadrupling the amount of the state's political power as well. Given the history of Texans' internal battles (including some that easily rival their more widely known external battles in size and scope), however, it is anything but a foregone conclusion that a Texas divided into four parts would think and act as one.

Modern Texans

Descendants of early Texas settlers have been the recipients of a rich and colorful history, more often than not passed on to them verbally by Texans with a uniquely Texan perspective. As one of the few states in America that mandates the teaching of the state's history in the public school system, Texas and the guardians of its heritage have always made sure that the children of the Lone Star state learn Texas history first, and U.S. history second. While the residents of most American states would be hard-pressed to name their state bird and flower, Texans needn't be prompted to point out a mockingbird in flight, or the bluebonnet in full bloom along a Texas roadway. Perhaps even more telling is the emotion and enthusiasm with which Texans belt out their state song, "Texas Our Texas."

THEIR MANNER OF DRESS is one of the many ways in which Texans express pride in their Western heritage.

NOT ALL COWBOYS WEAR TEN-GALLON HATS.

THOUGH LUCKENBACH IS a small town with only a handful of full-time inhabitants, they love to gather and celebrate their great town and their great state.

BRANDING CATTLE THE old-fashioned way is still the norm on the Y.O. Ranch (following page). While the days of cattle rustling are mostly gone, each ranch's distinctive brand still brings a source of pride to the ranch owner and workers.

In what surely must be a direct result of this rich oral historical tradition, the state of Texas has built a reputation for rearing individuals with sharp and well-honed tongues. In short, in its brief history, the state has turned out some rather eloquent practitioners of the Texas-accented English language... which is a nice way of saying that Texans have a proclivity toward fast talking.

While the expression "fast talker" may conjure up negative images to some, many Texans wear their naturally bred talent for speaking like a badge of courage. It is a fact that some of the great con men of all time have had Texas pedigrees. More ocean-front property has been sold in the Texas desert than in all of Florida, while countless fortunes have been lost drilling dry holes in mythical oil fields. None-theless, the few who have committed crimes of the speaking persuasion have been greatly outnum-bered by those who have put their tongues to positive uses. Some of America's most prominent journalists, including Walter Cronkite and Dan Rather, are proud natives of Texas and products of the state's public school system. The courtrooms of Texas have long been entertaining stages for tal-ented trial attorneys such as Percy Foreman, Richard "Racehorse" Haynes, and Joe Jamail. The state's pulpits are home to perhaps the most forceful speakers of Texas, the preachers and ministers of small rural churches. In the political arena, Texas has long gone unchallenged for superiority in the verbal wars fought in the political chambers of power. Sam Houston and Stephen F. Austin left tre-mendous legacies as a testament to the political power of the tongue. The persuasive nature of Lyn-don B. Johnson's "chats" over the many years of his political life are legendary, as are the oratorical skills of former Speaker of the House Jim Wright. Perhaps the greatest talent of mind and word in the state's history belongs to former Congresswoman Barbara Jordan, of Houston, the first African-American woman elected to Congress from Texas. The oratori-cal skills displayed by then Congresswoman Jordan during the Watergate hearings of the 1970s gave the rest of America the opportunity to hear one of the

THERE ARE THOUSANDS of celebrations each year in Texas, including one that salutes dirt, the Kolache Festival in Caldwell. Texans love to turn themselves out for a party, as this woman's party hat indicates (page 69).

MODERN-DAY TEXANS wear hats of many shapes and sizes, not just the legendary ten-gallon variety of frontier lore. Beards are another male-Texan tradition.

true golden voices of Texas. Now teaching at the Lyndon Baines Johnson School of Public Affairs at the University of Texas in Austin, the wisdom and insight of Professor Jordan is the private domain of a few fortunate students.

While some non-Texans are unimpressed, maybe even at times annoyed, by the oral tradition that Texans have known and continue to display, the tradition itself is alive and flourishing. In recent years, the people of Texas have refocused their efforts on a statewide level in order to raise the economic and educational standards of their state. As in years past, the heroes of the state have once again taken to the soap box in an effort to persuade their brethren of the need for such things as educational reform and economic diversification.

New leaders have emerged to carry forward into the next century the legacy of the founders of Texas. Henry Cisneros was elected the first Hispanic mayor of San Antonio in the early 1980s, and he led the city on a rapid course of modernization and economic expansion. Presently in business for himself, Cisneros is often mentioned as a future statewide, perhaps even national, officeholder. H. Ross Perot, founder of high-tech giant Electronic Data Systems Corporation, has played a leading role in educational reform and has provided the private funds needed to expand the state's share in national high-technology business. Kathy Whitmire, currently serving her third consecutive term as mayor of Houston, has led that city through difficult times, preparing it for a return to economic health and stability. Former State Treasurer Ann Richards arrived on the national political scene in fine Texas tradition by giving a rousing keynote speech to the 1988 Democratic National Convention. After a successful candidacy for Governor, she is the first woman to lead the state in over sixty years.

Any discussion of the people of Texas must include the accomplishments of the state's diverse ethnic community. Over fifty ethnic groups are represented in modern-day Texas. The most apparent ethnic influence in the state is a direct result of a long and close relationship with Texas' neighbor to the

MANY COWBOYS ARE JUST AS SERIOUS about making chili as they are about riding the range. These men give their all at a typical Texas chili cookoff.

A HOMETOWN TRIBUTE TO
the King of Texas rock and roll,
Charles Hardin "Buddy"
Holly, stands tall in Lubbock.
Although certainly the most
prolific singer and songwriter
to come out of Lubbock, Buddy
Holly was not the last. Mac
Davis, Joe Ely, and Delbert
McClinton are but a few of the
various talented musicians
who have hailed from the
Panhandle city.

GALVESTON'S TEMPERATE
climate and Gulf Coast location make it a popular spot for
water sports of all kinds. With
more than thirty miles (45 km)
of public beaches, and seven to
eight months of warm weather
and sunshine each year, fun in
the water around Galveston is
an almost year-round pursuit.

IRON EYES CODY HELPS
Texans recall and respect the contributions of Native Americans to the settlement of the Lone Star state.

THE TEXAN'S LOVE OF THE
active, outdoor life is evident in this woman's smile.

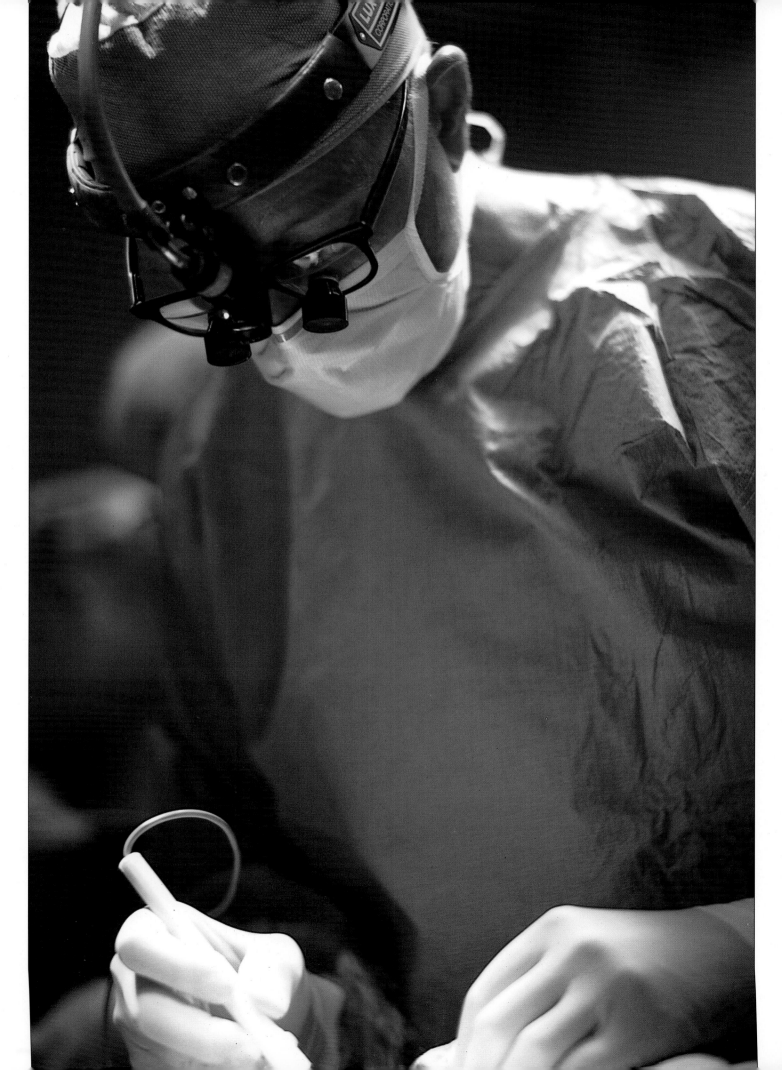

THE NEW PIONEERS OF THE Texas frontier are the gifted doctors and surgeons of the Texas Medical Center in Houston.

south, Mexico. For hundreds of years, the border that separates Texas and Mexico has proven less a barrier than a focal point for the meshing of two cultures. People and goods have traveled freely across the Rio Grande River, as have ideas and emotions. Hispanic Texans make up a full 20 percent of the state's population, a figure that is expected to grow with the results of the 1990 census. Texas and Mexico share more than a common river and a fifteen-hundred-mile (2,400-km) border. Indeed, they share each other. The great cities of Texas have prosperous and well-established Mexican-American communities, as do the more rural areas of South and West Texas. The border between the two countries is in fact difficult to define by its people, as the inhabitants of both areas are as apt to

speak Spanish as they are English; families on one side of the river are likely to have friends and relatives on the other side. The contributions of Mexican culture go far beyond the obvious influences on architecture, food, and language. As was the case a hundred and fifty years ago, Mexico and Texas are still the same in many respects.

While their numbers make up only about 12 percent of the population, African-Americans have made significant contributions to the state of Texas. The first African-Americans in Texas arrived as slaves of the Spanish explorers, more than four hundred years ago. Today, African-American communities in Houston and Dallas alone number in the hundreds of thousands. The intellectual genius of Houston's Barbara Jordan established a legacy for other

IT ONLY HAPPENS ONCE a year, but when the Washington Redskins come calling on the Dallas Cowboys, a city turns its undivided attention to sixty minutes of football.

African-Americans to follow, including the late Congressman Mickey Leland and his successor, Craig Washington. Contributions to the arts by African-Americans in Texas are significant and include the amazing work of native Texan Scott Joplin.

German immigrants arrived in Texas in around 1830 and brought with them lasting conservative values and ideals. Some of the very first public schools in Texas were established in the German communities of the Texas Hill Country. There are currently more than 700,000 people of German descent living in Texas, many in the Hill Country communities such as Fredericksburg and New Braunfels, which were founded by German immigrants. The German community in Texas takes great pride in native sons such as Chester W. Nimitz and Dwight D. Eisenhower.

One of the most recent ethnic groups to call Texas home are the 150,000 people of Asian origin living in the state. Significant among them are the flourishing community of Filipino professionals in Houston, and the prosperous group of Vietnamese fisherman along the Texas Gulf Coast.

While defining just exactly what is a Texan has become more difficult, defining what a Texan stands for has remained the same for hundreds of years. Just as the Texans of yesterday held fast to their feelings of independence and self-reliance, the Texans of today and tomorrow stand up and commit themselves to protecting that treasured legacy.

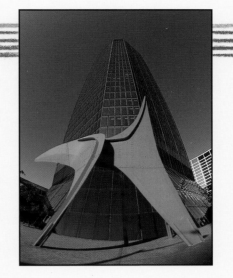

THE CITIES

In a letter written to U.S. President Andrew Jackson in 1832, General Sam Houston reported to his close friend that "there can be no doubt the country east and north of the Rio Grande River would sustain a population of ten million souls." Indeed, with a land mass almost one-fourth the size of the existing United States, it must have seemed to Houston that nearly all the people of America could have fit within the boundaries of Texas. While Houston's prediction would eventually prove true, not even he could have imagined that in time the state's five largest metropolitan areas combined would surpass ten million souls by themselves.

By the time Mexico assumed control of Texas in the early nineteenth century, centers of concentrated population had already begun to develop at several locations. San Antonio and Goliad in South Texas, and Nacogdoches in East Texas each had populations

THE OLDEST OF SAN *Antonio's five missions, and the oldest unreconstructed Catholic church in the United States, is Mission Concepcion, still offering Sunday mass in its two hundred and sixtieth year of service. The twin towers of the church make it easily recognizable in the San Antonio Missions National Historical Park.*

THE STATUE OF A WEST *Texas pioneer family, in Lubbock, expresses permanent gratitude to the settlers who tamed the wild plains of West Texas.*

of five thousand or more people. While the growth of San Antonio and Goliad was tied to the trade and commerce of their former (Spain) and present (Mexico) rulers, Nacogdoches was beginning to develop as an intermediate point for trade between Texas and the American South. At about the same time, the colonies that sprang from land grants obtained from Spain by Stephen F. Austin began to take root as well. With permission from the Spanish and Mexican governments, Austin had settled three hundred families in the fertile river beds of the Colorado and Brazos rivers. The colonies of Columbus and Washington prospered, each growing to around five thousand people. Due to their prosperity, as well as Austin's cooperation with Mexican authorities, the government of Mexico granted a substantial number of additional land grants to him over the course of the next ten years. These land

grants would prove to be the founding blocks of many communities across Texas, as settlers from the United States poured into the region to take advantage of cheap land and the chance to start a new life.

By the early 1830s, however, a growing number of disputes between established Mexican communities and new, primarily American settlements led the government of Mexico to halt the practice of giving land grants for legal settlement in Texas. American settlers continued to arrive, however, and the resulting rise in tensions set the events in motion for Texas' declaration of independence from Mexico. For the first time in its history, the vast land known as Texas was not big enough for everyone there to live in peace with one another.

Mexico's defeat at the hands of General Sam Houston and the army of Texas in 1836 freed the state of all rulers but itself. For the next ten years

Texas existed as a free and independent nation. The immigration of settlers from the U.S. and other, mostly European countries, continued. By the time Texas entered the United States in 1846, a large number of communities of several thousand people each had been firmly planted across the state.

While the towns of Texas continued to grow and prosper for the next fifty years, it was not until the discovery of a black gooey substance at the turn of the century that the state and its people were launched into a period of astronomical growth and urbanization.

It is an irony of history that the vast spaces of land that attracted so many settlers who came in search of isolation and solitude would provide the resources needed to create and maintain the great cities of Texas. With the discovery of oil in Southeast Texas, the state was set on an irreversible course of rapid growth and industrialization. By 1920, the population of Texas had surpassed four million. Areas of the state where cities once would have never been envisioned began to populate rapidly due to the exploration and refinement of petroleum and natural gas. Throughout the twentieth century, Texas has grown on a steady basis, unlike most American states with agriculture-based economies. By 1960, the state's population had reached ten million, and it nearly doubled in size again over the next twenty years.

▲   ▲   ▲   ▲

While the discovery of oil led to the creation of the state's first true metropolis in Houston, the financial spillover from the energy business created growth potential for the other cities of the state as well. It also provided the wealth needed to build the state's infrastructure, educational system, and cultural centers. With greater population and wealth came greater political power on a national and international level. Today, the state of Texas is home to three of the ten largest cities in America. In their own unique ways, Houston, Dallas, and San Antonio provide insight into the state's storied past, as well as distinct visions of the state's future.

SOARING INTO THE FUTURE, but ever mindful of the past, Sam Houston Park serves as a most appropriate front yard for the modern skyscrapers of downtown Houston. Preserved in the park are some of the oldest residential structures in the city, including the homes of some of Houston's founding fathers.

The city of Houston sits unrivaled as the world's energy capital, home to many of the largest oil and petrochemical companies on the globe. While this oil-related wealth has been somewhat depleted in recent years, Houston has become a center for medical and scientific research—an achievement that can be directly traced to the foresight and planning of the city's oil barons, who encouraged the growth of diversifying industries. Its stature as a center for artistic and cultural achievement can also be attributed to the generosity of the energy business. Founded in 1836 (appropriately enough as a speculative real estate development), the city was given its name shortly thereafter by the founding fathers of the Republic of Texas, to honor the hero of the battle of San Jacinto, General Sam Houston. Over the next 150 years, the original four thousand acres (1,600 ha) purchased by the Allen brothers in 1836 for less than $1.00 per acre (.4 ha), would serve as the foundation for the development of the fourth largest city in America.

True to the free and independent nature of Texans, the city of Houston has grown and sprawled in all directions, for the most part free of any zoning or planning constraints. With the discovery of oil near the turn of the century, followed by the construction of the ship channel in 1915 that linked the city with the Gulf of Mexico, Houston has been well equipped to serve as the energy capital of the world. Its stature in the international community has fueled one of the fastest growing urbanization rates in America's history, as well as providing the city with all of the requisite showcases that go along with rising to become a major global metropolis.

From a cultural standpoint, the city of Houston boasts an impressive array of artistic achievement, including dance, opera, and art. The city's Museum of Fine Arts boasts a permanent collection of works ranging from van Gogh and Matisse to Remington and Pollock. For devotees of more modern works, the Contemporary Arts Museum is a major repository for artistic pieces on the leading edge of the

REPOSITORIES OF ART AROUND THE state of Texas, such as the Museum of Fine Arts in Houston (pictured), have taken their rightful place alongside the outstanding art museums in the world. Designed by Mies van der Rohe, the Museum of Fine Arts houses a permanent collection that includes works by van Gogh, Matisse, and Picasso.

HOUSTON'S CONTEM-porary Arts Museum does not house the works of the older masters, as does its neighbor across the street, the Museum of Fine Arts. However, for admirers of the avant-garde in art, the "triangle coated in alu-minum," as the Contemporary Arts Museum is sometimes dubbed, displays contemporary works of equal importance.

A JOAN MIRÓ SCULPTURE in downtown Houston is one of many publicly commissioned artworks that graces the public spaces of Texas cities. Public spaces host all kinds of performances, including acrobatics.

RELICS DATING FROM prehistoric Texas are on display at the Museum of Natural Science in Houston. Situated in Hermann Park, the Museum offers interesting exhibits on the "black gold" that helped build the state.

avant-garde. In the area of the performing arts, few cities in the world can match the wide selection of venues available to the members and spectators of Houston's various performing groups. The Houston Grand Opera and the internationally touring Houston Ballet perform in the modern splendor of the Wortham Center, while the acoustical wonder of Jones Hall is a permanent home to the Houston Symphony and Houston Pops Orchestra. One of the oldest residential theatrical companies in America is the Alley Theatre, which has grown and prospered from its eponymous performance site (a small room in a back alley), to become a well-known theatrical company performing on two stages in a multi-million dollar production center.

As with all great cities, Houston's artistic accomplishments have been encouraged by generous benefactors, and appreciated by a general population with the desire to improve and enhance the quality of life in the community. Toward that end, the presence of major research institutions such as Rice University, Texas Southern University, and the University of Houston have helped the city grow by providing a steady flow of well-educated workers at all levels. One area in which Houston now has few rivals is in the delivery of medical services and medically related research and development. The two-hundred-acre (80-ha) campus of the Texas Medical Center is home to over twenty-five major health facilities, including the Baylor College of Medicine,

EXPLORING NEW FRONTIERS continues to be a Texas trademark. The Johnson Space Center, near Houston, plays a vital role in America's quest to reveal the mysteries of the stars. Most parts of the Space Center, including the legendary Mission Control, are open to visitors.

WHEN THE REAL THING JUST WON'T DO, BULL RIDERS OF ALL SORTS
have tried their skill at Gilley's Nightclub in Pasadena. Immortalized in the movie
Urban Cowboy, *the genuine Texas honky-tonk currently sits idle.*

THE SAN JACINTO MONUment is aglow every April twenty-first in celebration of Texas Independence, and of course every fourth of July in celebration of American Independence.

93

various general hospitals, and numerous specialty centers where medical miracles are performed on a daily basis.

The Houston of yesterday is known to many as little more than an oilman's town. The Houston of today and tomorrow, however, is being forged in the classrooms of its first-rate universities, and in the technologically advanced operating rooms of its medical centers. In many ways, the Houston Astrodome, built in 1965 and immediately labeled the Eighth Wonder of the World, set the tone for what was to follow. With the establishment of NASA's LBJ Space Center, Houston soon became home to the American effort at conquering outer space, and set itself on a course to achieve equal status with the great cities of the world. Houston's race toward the future, most symbolically displayed by the gleaming skyscrapers of its central business district, might give the impression that the city is anxious to shed its Texas image. Quite to the contrary, however, Houston and Houstonians remain anxious to reveal their vision of Texas' future.

Dallas

Although it is clear that not all of the cities of Texas owe their existence to energy, the state's natural resources and the wealth they created have nevertheless played a crucial role in urbanizing the once mostly rural state. The city of Dallas has soared in stature as a center for global commerce and trade, due in large part to a carefully fostered environment favorable to the conducting of business. While the growth of the city has receded in recent years in response to the slumping energy business, efforts at diversifying the area's economy have provided some insulation from the devastating effects felt by the energy-dependent cities and towns of the "Oil Patch."

Through the enterprising efforts of the city's residents and business leaders, Dallas has grown from its origins as a small trading post founded on the banks of the Trinity River in 1841 to America's seventh largest city, with over one million residents.

THE FUTURISTIC SKYLINE of downtown Dallas makes a forceful statement that the city has assumed its place as a major center of trade and commerce in America.

95

NOT EVEN HOLLYWOOD CAN OUTDO THE REAL THING WHEN IT COMES TO
*capturing the sprawling grandeur of a working Texas ranch. Getting up close to a real ranch
is made easier in the Dallas–Ft. Worth area by the presence of several "dude" ranches
open to the public.*

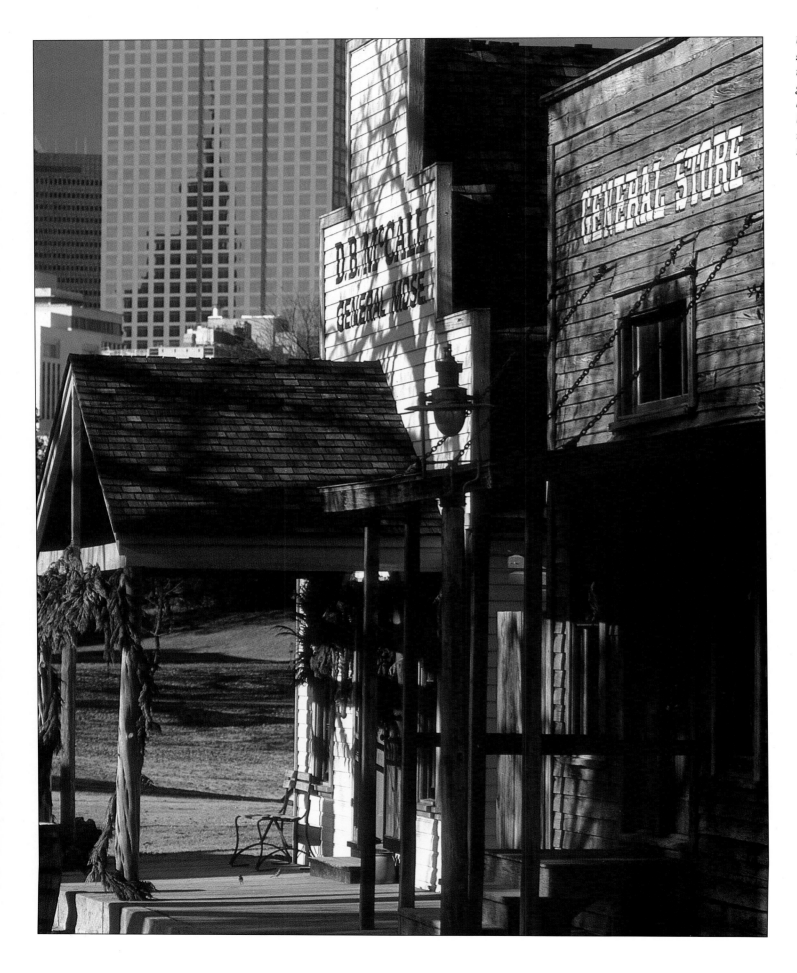

97

UNDER THE GLEAMING shadow of a Dallas skyscraper, the Old City Park helps younger generations learn how their ancestors lived. The thirty buildings in the park form a museum depicting life in Texas since the pre-Civil War period.

ONCE KNOWN AS THE GATEWAY to the rest of America for ranchers and their cattle, Fort Worth now serves as a gateway to commerce and industry in Texas. The city that once was second only to Chicago in the size of its stockyards now serves as a corporate home to various high-technology companies.

The Metroplex, encompassing Dallas and Fort Worth as well as hundreds of suburban communities, now contains over three million residents in its metropolitan area. As a testament to the city's concerted efforts at fostering a positive business environment, Dallas now ranks third in the nation in the number of multi-million-dollar companies that call the city home. The city is also a major center of such diverse industries as fashion, insurance, and filmmaking. Dallas has the largest merchandise mart in the world, and is also home to the largest cotton trading center in America. Perhaps the greatest trophy of all is the Dallas-Fort Worth Regional Airport, in size the largest airport in America, trailing only Chicago and Atlanta in the number of daily arrivals and departures.

As in Houston to the south, the residents of Dallas have gone to great lengths to endow their city with impressive cultural facilities, including world-class ballet and opera companies. Unlike Houston, however, the establishment of the major Arts District in downtown Dallas has been a citywide undertaking, funded equally by public support and private donations. The crown jewels of the Arts District are the Dallas Museum of Art, opened in 1984 and now housing a permanent collection that includes works by Gauguin and Picasso; and the I.M. Pei-designed Morton H. Meyerson Symphony Center, which opened to rave technical reviews in 1989. The funding and construction of the $100 million Meyerson Center, home to the Dallas Symphony Orchestra, provides solid evidence of the city's desire to accept nothing short of equal cultural status with the great cities of the world.

MANY OUTSTANDING artistic chronicles of America's westward expansion are housed and displayed at the Amon Carter Museum of Western Art in Fort Worth. Although the works of many artists are on display at the Amon Carter, the main focus and spirit of the museum's permanent collection are the paintings and sculptures of Americans Charles Russell and Frederic Remington.

A CITY AS OLD AS THE state itself, the modern Fort Worth now sits proudly next to its neighbor, Dallas. While competition between Dallas and Fort Worth does exist, the explosion in growth in the Metroplex area can be directly attributed to cooperation among the leaders and residents of both cities.

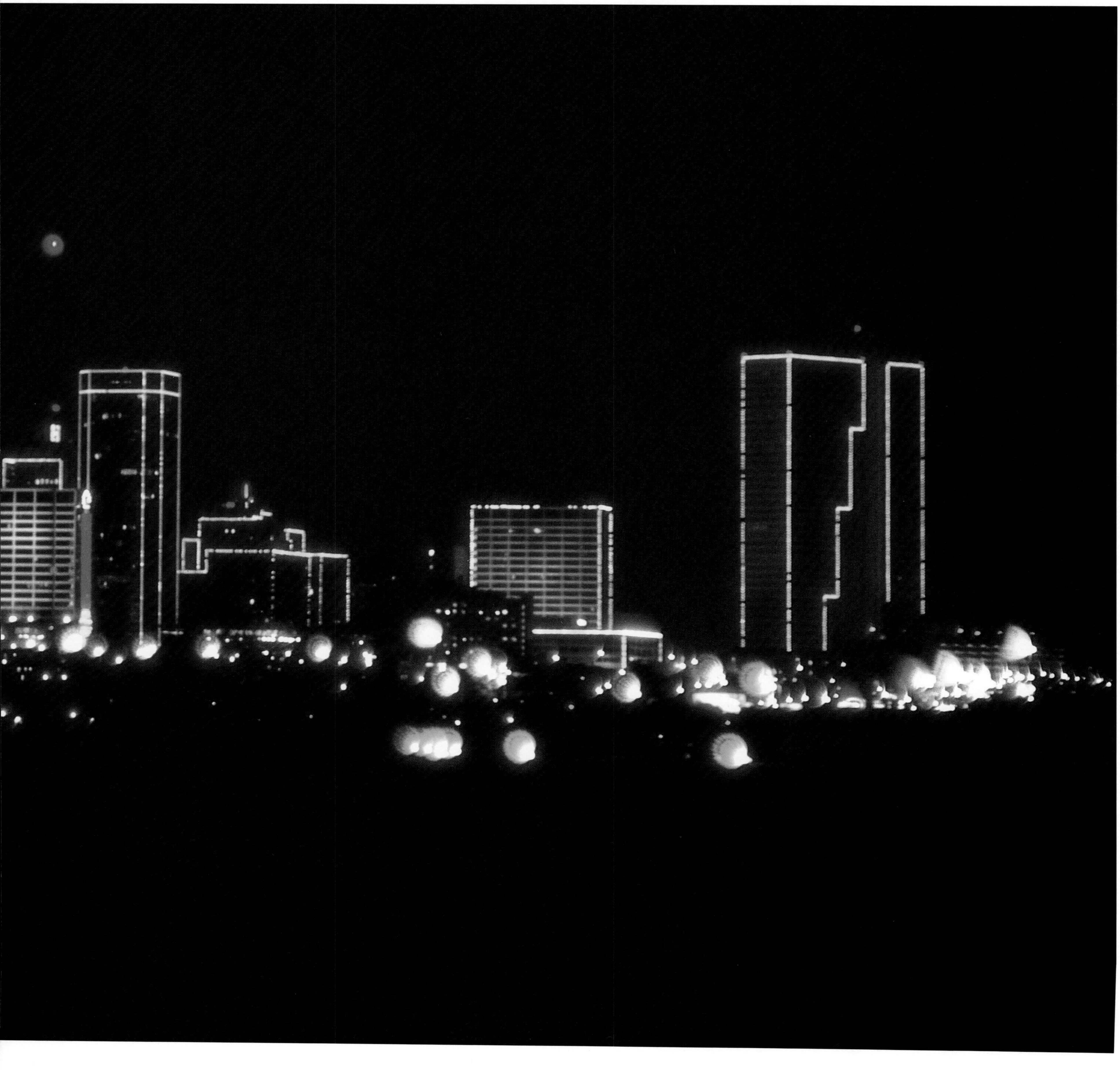

San Antonio

Uniting the state's past with its future is the beautiful city of San Antonio. As the oldest center of population in the state, San Antonio has grown and prospered through every period of the state's settlement. Spanish and Mexican influences are an integral part of the city's history. With a Hispanic population making up almost half of the metropolitan area's 1.3 million people, the lasting influences of the region's historical association with Spain and Mexico form a vital part of the city's fabric.

It is not only the history of San Antonio that sets it apart from other Texas cities, but the respect that its residents have for the past. The "If it's old, tear it down" attitude prevalent in Dallas and Houston is anathema to the citizens of San Antonio. Spanish explorers were known to be in the area of modern-day San Antonio as early as the late seventeenth century. The city had been founded by 1718, its name taken from the small meandering river on the banks of which the village had been settled—San Antonio de Padua. Unlike the residents of most cities in Texas, and in America for that matter, San Antonians are very aware of, and very eager to share their knowledge of the city's history. It is this awareness of and appreciation for history that has led to the preservation of a great part of the city's past. These efforts at historical preservation have made San Antonio the leading destination of choice for Texans not lucky enough to call the city home.

San Antonio has a strong military presence with four Air Force bases and a major Army installation—one source of the city's economic stability. Tourism provides the city with another stable and lucrative industry that feeds off the area's charm and history. Appropriately enough, the most famous of all the city's attractions, the Alamo and the Paseo de Rio, are vital links to the city's past. Built at the time of San Antonio's founding, the Mission San Antonio de Valero survives today in the form of the chapel and surrounding grounds, known to all simply as the Alamo. Although the four missions built in the decade following the Alamo's construction (Con-

A LINK TO SAN ANTONIO's past is the carefully restored Spanish Governor's Palace (previous page), built in 1749 to house the caretaker of Spain's far flung empire in present day South Texas. Now carefully restored with furniture from the period, the palace and its Spanish courtyard are open to visitors.

MISSION ESPADA, ONE OF five missions built by Franciscan missionaries on the banks of the San Antonio River. Still in use on the mission grounds is an aqueduct, built in the early 1730s, as a reliable irrigation system.

THERE IS NO PLACE MORE SACRED TO NATIVE TEXANS THAN THE MISSION SAN Antonio de Valero, more commonly known as the Alamo. Built as the mission's chapel, the Alamo served as the final stand for one hundred eighty-seven brave men who put Texas on a course toward independence from Mexico in 1836.

THE SYMBOLIC HOME OF the "national beer of Texas" is the Lone Star Brewery in San Antonio. Like so many of the state's treasures, Lone Star beer is now in the hands of non-Texans, otherwise known as foreigners. However, business continues "as usual", with sales rung up on this classic cash register.

cepcion, San Jose, San Juan Capistrano, and San Francisco de la Espada) offers a more spiritual and aesthetic presence, the small chapel of the Mission San Antonio de Valero holds historical significance for all Texans. It was here that a small number of Texan volunteers died at the hands of an overwhelming Mexican Army in 1836, an event that inspired the state's drive toward independence from Mexico. The chapel is now preserved and maintained by the direct descendants of the heroes of the Alamo and Texas Independence, the Daughters of the Republic of Texas. While the Alamo's storied past has made it the number one historical attraction in the state of Texas, visitors to the city should not miss the beauty of the other missions, now preserved in the San Antonio Missions National Historic Park.

The city's other main attraction, the Paseo del Rio (Riverwalk), also shares in the city's past. The San Antonio River provided the Spanish explorers with the water they needed to support human settlement. Almost three hundred years later, a tiny two-mile (3-km) stretch of the river provides San Antonio with a focal point for natives and visitors alike. Today, the winding banks of the downtown stretch of the river are shaded by stately oak and cypress trees that shelter the various shops and sidewalk cafés that dot the Paseo del Rio. Food, music, and people make the Riverwalk a delightful stop during any visit to the Alamo City. The Paseo del Rio also serves the purpose of tying several downtown attractions together. In addition to providing access to the Alamo and most major hotels, the Riverwalk also leads to La Villita, an area of restored homes, some dating back as far as the mid-1700s; and to Hemisfair Plaza, the sight of the 1968 World's Fair. Today, La Villita serves as a year-round home to various artisans who display their wares inside the same adobe walls that housed some of San Antonio's original residents. It is also the site of "A Night in Old San Antonio," one of the major events in the city's annual weeklong celebration known as Fiesta. Although it sat virtually unused for many years after the World's Fair in 1968, Hem-

THE HISTORIES OF THE PEOPLE WHO turned the Texas Panhandle into a fertile and productive region are on display at the Ranching Heritage Center in Lubbock.

isfair Plaza is now a center for various cultural and educational institutions, including the Institute of Texan Cultures (which holds the annual Texas Folklife Festival), and the National Autonomous University of Mexico.

While San Antonio has not shared in the great oil-related wealth bestowed upon Houston and Dallas, the city's residents have made every effort at keeping pace with the cultural aspirations of their larger and wealthier neighbors. The San Antonio Museum of Art sits in the restored splendor of the former Lone Star Brewery. Among the more notable aspects of its permanent collection is a renowned assemblage of Mexican folk art. For more traditional art lovers, the McNay Art Institute contains works by Cezanne, Gauguin, and Picasso, within the walls of a restored Spanish style mansion. Visitors looking for excitement beyond the city's historical and artistic attractions will find plenty of enjoyment at the San Antonio Zoo, where over three thousand specimens of animals are displayed in their natural habitats, and at the recently opened Sea World of Texas.

Other Cities

Lubbock, founded in 1876 and named after Colonel Tom S. Lubbock, is the world's largest cottonseed processing center. The city is also the center of the agribusiness in the state. Tourist attractions include a Ranching Heritage Center located on the campus

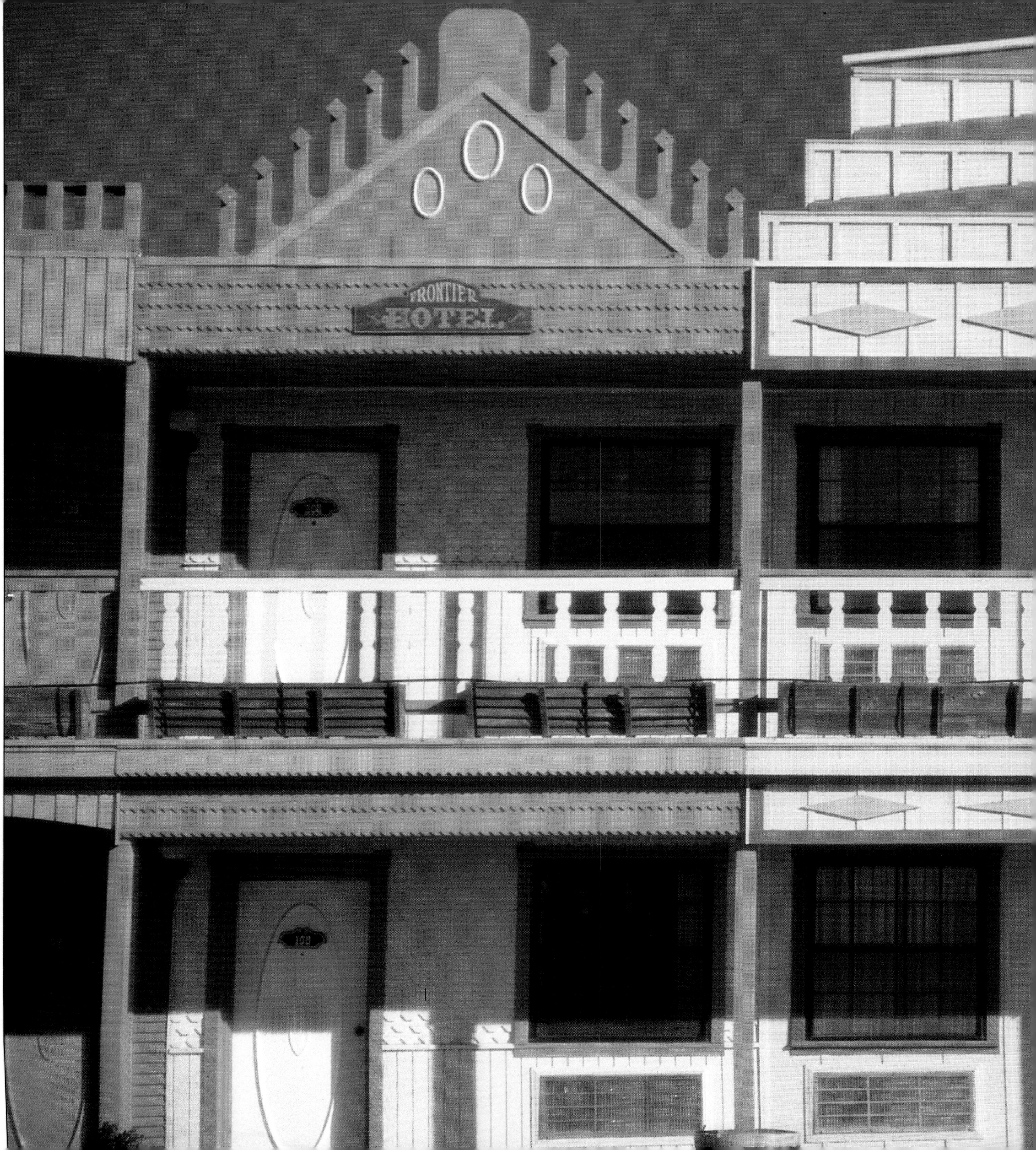
FRONTIER
HOTEL
209
109

*BIG IN NAME ONLY,
the Big Texan Motel offers a
splash of color across the High
Plains of Texas near Amarillo.*

IN THE CENTER OF MAIN STREET IN Lajitas sits the Badlands Hotel, welcoming visitors to the Big Bend area of West Texas. If you don't check in here, you've got a very long drive to the next hotel.

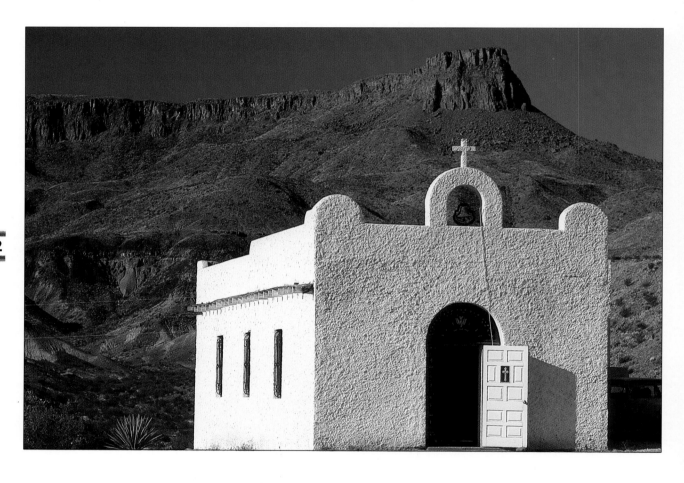

THE MOUNTAINS AND DESERTS OF WEST TEXAS ARE DOTTED WITH THE WHITE STUCCO EXTERIORS OF MANY "cathedrals." The style and design of these houses of worship have changed very little over the last several hundred years.

THE BIG BLUE SKY OF the Texas Panhandle sets an appropriate backdrop for one Texan's vision of ranching... Cadillac style.

114

of Texas Tech University, where the structures and culture of the High Plains settlers have been preserved. The Lubbock Lake archaeological site is one of the most interesting in the state, providing a glimpse of life—both human and animal—on the South Plains that dates back to the Pleistocene era.

Amarillo was established as a cattle shipping center in 1887, as the railroads opened up the Texas Panhandle. Today it is the thriving urban hub for North Panhandle oil, and a marketing and distribution center for a five-state area. Palo Duro Canyon State Park, a popular tourist attraction, presents a summer musical, "Texas," in the outdoor Pioneer Amphitheater. Abilates Flint Quarries and Texas Panhandle Pueblo Culture National Monument are also located there.

Fort Worth, whose motto, "Where the West Begins," has grown from a frontier outpost to a bustling city. Seven major railroads connect there, making it a shipping hub for the Southwest. With eight colleges and universities, a number of museums, and the gigantic western nightclub known as "Billy Bob's Texas," Fort Worth has much to offer visitors.

Galveston, one of Texas' most historic cities, was founded in 1838, and named for the Spanish governor of Louisiana, Count Bernardo de Galvez. Pirates once used the island as a base from which to raid in the Gulf. It remains an important port today. Galveston's warm climate, 32-mile (51-km) Gulf beach, Historic District, and festivals such as the Shrimp Festival attract large numbers of visitors. In the summer, the drama "Lone Star" is presented in Mary Moody Northern Amphitheater in Galveston Island State Park.

Corpus Christi is a major port and center for petrochemical production. A naval air station and army base are located in the city. The warm waters of Corpus Christi Bay and the Gulf of Mexico are popular with sailors, surfers, anglers, and other water sport lovers, and annual events include Buccaneer Days, a jazz festival, and a deep-sea round-up. Corpus Christi also serves as the gateway to Padre Island National Seashore.

115

FOR MORE THAN ONE hundred years, one of the most handsome residents of Galveston's historic Strand District has been the luxurious Tremont House hotel. Its one hundred twenty-five luxurious rooms have housed the rich and famous in Victorian splendor since well before the turn of the century.

THE WEALTHY MERCHANTS and traders of Galveston's past left a treasure of architectural gems as proof of their free-spending days. As home to more than five hundred registered structures of historical significance, including many private residences, Galveston is an architecture lover's paradise.

Brownsville rests at the southern tip of Texas. With a semi-tropical climate, the area is one of the nation's leading vegetable and citrus fruit producers. Its Gulf location makes it a tourist center as well, with year-round events such as Charro Days in February and RioFest in March. The Gladys Porter Zoo for Endangered Species and the Confederate Air Force Museum are must-sees.

Austin, the state capital, is a center for state government, tourism, and technological industries. The central campus of the University of Texas is found in Austin, as are a number of other educational institutions. Attractions include the State Capitol, the Governor's Mansion, and Lyndon B. Johnson Presidential Library. Nearby are the LBJ Ranch and State Park, numerous Colorado River lakes, and the scenic Texas Hill Country.

While oil-generated wealth spurred the urbanization of Houston and Southeast Texas, the land contained other resources to be developed that contributed to the growth of cities throughout Texas. The vast abundance of suitable grazing and farming lands provided the foundations for the establishment of many agricultural empires, which in turn led to the development of population centers geared toward the processing and transportation of agricultural products. The cities of Lubbock and Amarillo in the Texas Panhandle developed as centers of trade and commerce for the cotton and ranching kingdoms of the Texas High Plains, while the city of Fort Worth went unrivaled for many years as America's hub for the transportation of livestock and related products. The resources of the land and ocean gave rise to cities along the Gulf Coast, as Galveston, Corpus Christi, and later, Brownsville, grew in size and stature as ports of embarkation for Texas-made goods and products.

While there may be disagreement among Texans as to which city best represents Texas, one thing is for certain: From the historical allure of San Antonio to the modernistic megopolises of Houston and Dallas, the cities of Texas were forged from the same land, by the same people, and most importantly of all, with the same spirit.

119

SCATTERED ALL OVER
Texas are examples of the indigenous adobe architecture, such as this complex near El Paso.

THE FLAMINGOS STRIKE A COLORFUL *pose at the Gladys Porter Zoo, in Brownsville. The temperate weather of the Rio Grande Valley makes it possible to keep the Zoo's impressive collection of animals outdoors on a year-round basis.*

RENOWNED FOR ITS SUCCESS IN RECREATING THE NATURAL SETTINGS FOR HUNDREDS OF *endangered animals, the Gladys Porter Zoo, in Brownsville, is a popular stop for visitors from both sides of the border.*

*THE FRONT PORCH OF THE
Gruene Inn offers a warm and
friendly invitation to experience life as it was in a more
simple past.*

PROSPEROUS TIMES HAVE LEFT PERMANENT IMPRINTS ON THE TEXAS landscape. A Pompeiian Villa in Port Arthur is one of many examples of Texans' efforts to bring some of the rest of the world back to their home state.

APPENDIX

Further Reading

Texas State Travel Guide
c/o State Department of Highways
P.O. Box 5064
Austin, Texas 78763
(512) 465-7401
Highway and park guide

Bed and Breakfast Texas Style
4224 West Red Bird Lane
Dallas, Texas 75237
(214) 298-5433
Pamphlet on Texas bed and breakfasts

Hill County Tourism Association
1001 Junction Highway
Kerrville, Texas 78028
(512) 895-5000
Pamphlet on dude ranches

Lower Colorado River Authority
3700 Lake Austin Boulevard
Box 220
Austin, Texas 78767
Pamphlet on boating

Guide to Texas Hunting and Fishing
Texas Parks and Wildlife Department
4200 Smith School Road
Austin, Texas 78744
(800) 792-1112
Pamphlet on the hunting and fishing regulations

Sources

Greater Houston Convention and
Visitors Council
3300 South Main
Houston, Texas 77002
(800) 231-7799

Galveston Convention and Visitors Bureau
2106 Seawall Boulevard
Galveston, Texas
(800) 351-4237

Corpus Christi Area Convention
and Visitors Bureau
1201 North Shoreline
P.O. Box 2664
Corpus Christi, Texas 78403
(800) 678-6232

Dallas Convention and Visitors Bureau
1201 Elm Street
Dallas, Texas 75270
(214) 746-6677

Fort Worth Convention and Visitors Bureau
100 East 15th Street
Suite 400
Fort Worth, Texas 76102
(817) 336-8791

Austin Convention and Visitors Bureau
Box 2990
Austin, Texas 78769
(512) 478-0098

San Antonio Convention and Visitors
Bureau
P.O. Box 2277
San Antonio, Texas 78298
(800) 447-3372

El Paso Convention and Visitors Bureau
P.O. Box 9738
El Paso, Texas 79901
(915) 534-0698

INDEX

Page numbers in italics refer to captions and photographs.

Abilates Flint Quarries (Amarillo), 115
Adams, John Quincy, 10
Adobe architecture, *119*
African-Americans, 79-80
Agriculture
 in North Texas, 19-27
 in Panhandle, 28
Alamo, *56*, 57-60, 103-7, *105*
Alley Theater (Houston), 91
Alvarez de Pineda, Alonzo, 10
Amarillo, 115
 as cotton and ranching center, 118
American High Plains, 28
Amon Carter Museum of Western Art (Fort Worth), *99*
Aransas Pass, *43*
Arapaho Indians, 54
Architecture
 adobe, *119*
 "cathedrals," *112*
Army of the Republic of Texas, *55*
Arts
 in Dallas, 99
 in Houston, 87-91
 oil money and, 44
 in San Antonio, 108

Arts District (Dallas), 99
Asian immigrants, 80
Austin, 118
Austin, Stephen F., 57-60, 68, 84

Badlands Hotel, *112-13*
Bald eagle, *16-17*
Balli, Jose Nicolas, 41
Baron's Creek Inn, *80*
Baylor College of Medicine, 91
Beards, as male tradition, *71*
Big Bend National Park, 32
Big Bend region, *32-33*
Big Texan Motel, *111*
Big Thicket region, 14
Bilingualism, 79
Billy Bob's Texas (nightclub), 115
Bluebonnets, *30-31*, 65
Bowie, James, 57
Brownsville, 118
Buccaneer Days (festival), 115
Buffalo, ranches as preserves for, *26*

Cacti, 32, *36*
Caddo Lake, 14-19
Candelilla plant, 32
"Cathedrals," style and design, *112*
Cattle
 branding, *67-68*

Texas Longhorn, 24-25
Cattle drives, *58*
Cattle ranches, *22-23*, 49
Charreada, *58-59*
Charro Days (festival), 118
Chili cookoffs, *72-73*
Cisneros, Henry, 72
Cities
 development and growth of, 83-85
 oil in rise of, 85
 See also specific cities
Claret cup flower, *36*
Coastal Texas, 41
Cody, Iron Eyes, *76-77*
Columbus (colony), 84
Comanche Indians, 54
Con artists, 68
Concepcion Mission (San Antonio), 103-7
Confederate Air Force Museum (Brownsville), 118
Contemporary Arts Museum (Houston), 87-91, *88*
Corn, as agricultural staple, 27
Corpus Christi, 115
 as shipping center, 118
Cotton, as agricultural staple, 27
Cowboys, *61*, *72-73*
Creosote bush, 32
Crockett, David, 57
Cronkite, Walter, 68

Crosbyton Solar Power Project, *50*
Cultural attractions
 in Dallas, 99
 in Houston, 87-91
 in San Antonio, 108
Culture, oil money and, 44

Dallas
 business environment of, 99
 as commerce and trade center, 94, *98*
 cultural attractions, 99
 growth of, 94
 Metroplex, 99, *100*
 skyline, *95*
Dallas Cowboys (football team), *79*
Dallas-Fort Worth Regional Airport, 99
Dallas Museum of Art, 99
Dallas Symphony Orchestra, 99
Dam construction, 19
Daughters of the Republic, *56*, 107
Davis, Mac, *74*
Davy Crockett National Forest, *15*
"Day in Old Mexico" fiesta, *58-59*
de Galvez, Bernardo, 115
Deserts
 flora, *36-37*
 of West Texas, 32

de Vaca, Cabeza, 10
Dress styles, *65, 66, 71*
Dude ranches, *96*

East Texas
 flora and fauna, 19
 geography, 14
 lakes and rivers, 19
Economy
 cattle breeding, 49
 diversification, 49
 oil in, 44-49
Educational mandate, 65
Eisenhower, Dwight D., 80
Electronic Data Systems Corporation, 72
Elevation, 8
Elissa (ship), *40-41*
El Paso, *119*
Ely, Joe, *74*
Ethnic diversity, 72-80
 in San Antonio, 103
Exploration, 10

Falcon Lake, *42*
Fashion, *65, 66, 71*
Fauna
 coastal, 29
 of desert, 32
 in East Texas, 14
 of East Texas, 19
Filipino immigrants, 80
Fishing, on Rio Grande River, *42*
Flora
 bluebonnets, *30-31*, 65

125

of desert, 32, *36-37*
  of East Texas, 14, 19
Foreman, Percy, 68
Forests, of East Texas, 19
Fort Worth, 115
  as cattle transport
    center, 118
  Metroplex, 99, *100*
Fredericksburg, 80
French expansion, 10
Future Farmers of
  America, *60*

Galveston, *74-75*, 115
  architectural features,
    117
  historic district, *116*
  maritime history, *40-41*
  as shipping center, 118
Galveston Historical
  Foundation, *40-41*
Geography, 9
  coast, 29
  coastal, 41
  East Texas, 14
  Panhandle, 28
  West Texas, 32
Geology, in Palo Duro
  Canyon, 29
German immigrants, 80
Gilley's Nightclub
  (Pasadena), *92*
Gladys Porter Zoo for
  Endangered Species
  (Brownsville), 118, *120-21*
Goliad, at time of Mexican
  control, 83-84
Gorman Falls, *17*
Governor's Mansion, 118
Governor's Palace (San
  Antonio), *103-4*
Grain, as agricultural
  staple, 27
Gruene Inn, *122*
Guadalupe Mountains
  National Park, *8, 11*
Guadalupe Peak, *11,* 32
Gulf of Mexico, 14, 41

Hats, *66, 71*
Haynes, Richard, 68
Hemisfair Plaza (San
  Antonio), 107-8
Hermann Park (Houston),
  90

High Plains of Texas, *111*
Hill Country, *14*
Hispanic Texans, 79
  in San Antonio, 103
Holly, Buddy, *74*
Horses, as transportation,
  34
Houston
  cultural attractions,
    87-91
  founding and
    development of, 87
  oil and, 87
  universities and research
    institutes, 91-94
Houston, Samuel, *55, 57,*
  60, 68, 83, 84, 87
Houston Astrodome, 94
Houston Ballet, 91
Houston Grand Opera, 91
Houston Pops Orchestra,
  91
Houston Symphony, 91

Independence Trail, *55*
Institute of Texan Culture
  (San Antonio), 108

Jackson, Andrew, 83
Jamail, Joe, 68
Jefferson, Thomas, 57
Johnson, Lyndon B., 68
  ranch, *27,* 118
Johnson Space Center, *91,*
  94
Jones Hall (Houston), 91
Joplin, Scott, 80
Jordan, Barbara, *68-72,* 79

Karankawa Indians, 41
King Ranch, 49
Kiowa Indians, 54
Kolache Festival, *71*

Lafitte, Jean, 41
Laguna Madre, 41
Lajitas, *112-13*
Lake Amistad, *42*
Lake Livingston, 19
Lakes
  in East Texas, 19
  See also specific lakes
Land, size, 9, 44
Land grants, in
  development of Texas, 84

La Villita (San Antonio),
  107
L.B.J. Ranch, *27,* 118
Leland, Mickey, 80
Lincoln, Abraham, 57
Llano Estacado Canyon,
  28
Loetscher, Ila, *41, 64*
Lone Star Brewery, *106,*
  108
Lone Star Feed Yard, *22*
Longhorn steers, *24-25, 48*
Louisiana Purchase, 10
Louisiana Territories, 10
Lubbock, 108, 115
  as cotton and ranching
    center, 118
Lubbock, Tom S., 108
Lubbock Lake
  archaeological site, 115
Luckenbach, *67*
Lyndon B. Johnson
  Presidential Library, 118
Lyndon Johnson Space
  Center, *51*

McClinton, Delbert, *74*
McNay Art Institute (San
  Antonio), 108
Mary Moody Northern
  Amphitheater
  (Galveston), 115
Metroplex (Dallas/Fort
  Worth), 99, *100*
Mexico
  Alamo and
    independence from,
    107
  Austin's dealings with,
    57-60
  border with, *39*
  cultural influence of, 79,
    103
  development of cities
    under jurisdiction of,
    83-84
  independence from, 60,
    84-85
  Texas under jurisdiction
    of, 10
Mission Concepcion, *84*
Mission Espada (San
  Antonio), *104*
Missions, in San Antonio,
  103-7

Mission San Antonio de
  Valero. *See* Alamo
Mockingbird, 65
Morton H. Meyerson
  Symphony Center, 99
Mountains, of Big Bend
  region, *32-33*
Museum of Fine Arts
  (Houston), 87, *88*
Museum of Natural
  Science (Houston), *90*

Nacogdoches, at time of
  Mexican control, 83-84
National Autonomous
  University of Mexico,
  108
Native Americans, 54
  contributions to Texas
    settlement by,
    76-77
  early settlers and, 57
  prior to European
    settlement, 29
  *See also specific Native-
  American groups*
Neches River, 14
New Braunfels, 80
"A Night in Old San
  Antonio" (celebration),
  107
Nimitz, Chester W., 80
North Texas, agriculture,
  19-27

Oil, 44-49
  rise of cities and
    discovery of, 85
Old City Park (Dallas), *97*
Oral history tradition,
  65-68
Oratorical tradition, 68-72

Padre Island National
  Seashore, 41, 115
Palo Duro Canyon, 28, 29,
  115
Panhandle, 28
Paseo del Rio (San
  Antonio), 103, 107
Peanuts, as agricultural
  staple, 27
Permian Basin Petroleum
  Museum, *45*
Perot, H. Ross, 72

Piney Woods region, 14,
  18-19
Pioneer Amphitheater
  (Amarillo), 115
Political leadership, 72
Port Arthur, *123*
Port Isabel, 41
Prickly pear, *37*

Rainfall, in desert, 32
Ranches, 22-23, *114*
  as buffalo preserves, *26*
  dude, *96*
  L.B.J., *27,* 118
Ranching Heritage Center
  (Lubbock), *31, 108,* 108,
  115
Rather, Dan, 68
Red River, 14
Regions
  Coastal, 29
  coastal, 41
  East Texas, 14-19
  North Texas, 19-27
  Panhandle, 28
  West Texas, 32
Remington, Frederic, *99*
Research institutes, in
  Houston, 91-94
Resources, 44-49
  cattle, 49
Rice, as agricultural staple,
  27
Rice University, 91
Richards, Ann, 72
Rio Grande River, 32
  fishing on, *42*
  as Texas-Mexico border,
    39
Rivers
  in East Texas, 19
  See also specific rivers
Rodeos, *58-59*
  children's training for, *60*
Russell, Charles, *99*

Sabine River, 14
  dam construction along,
    19
Sam Houston Day, *52, 54*
Sam Houston Park, *86*
San Antonio
  attractions, 107-8
  cultural attractions, 108
  historical attractions, 103-7

Mexican influence in, 103
reverence for history in, 103
settlement and growth of, 103
at time of Mexican control, 83-84
San Antonio Missions National Historical Park, *84*, 107
San Antonio Museum of Art, 108
San Antonio River, 107
San Antonio Zoo, 108
San Francisco de la Espada Mission (San Antonio), 107
San Jacinto, battle of, 60
San Jacinto Monument, *93*
San Jose Mission (San Antonio), 107

San Juan Capistrano Mission (San Antonio), 107
Santa Anna, 60
Sea turtles, 41, *64*
Sea World of Texas, 108
Seminole Canyon State Park, *29*
Settlement, early, 54-60
Shrimp Festival, 115
Shrimp industry, *43*
Slavery, 79
Soybeans, as agricultural staple, 27
Space exploration, Texas-based facilities for, *51*
Spanish exploration, 10
State bird, 65
State Capitol building, 118
State flower, *30-31*, 65
Statehood, 60
annexation agreement, 65

State song, 65
Strand District (Galveston), *116*
Superconducting Supercollider, future development in Texas of, 49

Texas
annexation agreement, 65
early settlers, 54-60
historical rulers, 53-54
mentality of people, 53
size, 9, 44
statehood, 60, 65
state pride, 54
Texas Folklife Festival, 108
Texas Longhorn, *24-25*, *48*
Texas Medical Center, *78*, 91-94
"Texas Our Texas" (state song), 65
Texas Panhandle Pueblo

Culture National Monument, 115
Texas Rangers, *62*
Texas Southern University, 91
Texas Tech University, 115
Texas Youth Rodeo Association, *60*
Toledo Bend Reservoir, 19
Town gatherings, *67*
Transportation, horses for, *34*
Travis, William B., 57
Trees, in East Texas, 19
Tremont House Hotel (Galveston), *116*
Trinity River, 14
dam construction along, 19
Turtles, 41, *64*

Universities, in Houston, 91-94
University of Houston, 91

University of Texas, 118
Urban Cowboy (movie), *92*

van der Rohe, Mies, *88*
Vietnamese immigrants, 80

Wagon trains, *54*
Washington (colony), 84
Washington, Craig, 80
Washington, George, 57
Washington Redskins (football team), *79*
Water sports, *74-75*
West Texas, 32
Wheat, as agricultural staple, 27
Whitmire, Kathy, 72
Wortham Center (Houston), 91
Wright, Jim, 68

Y.O. Ranch, *48*, *49*, *67-68*

127